WRITING WORKBOOK for kids with Dyslexia

100 activities to improve writing and reading skills of dyslexic children

Volume 5

BrainChild

Copyright 2020 - All Rights Reserved

Contents of this book may not be reproduced, duplicated or transmitted without direct written permission from the author. Under no circumstances will any legal responsibility or blame be held against the publisher for any reparation, damages or monetary loss due to information herein, either directly or indirectly.

Legal Notice

You cannot amend, distribute, sell, use, quote or paraphrase any part of the contents within this book without the consent of the author.

Disclaimer Notice

Please note that the information contained within this document serves only for educational and entertainment purposes only. No warranties of any kind are expressed or implied. Readers acknowledge that the author is not engaging in the rendering of legal, financial, medical or professional advice.

Table of Contents

Copyright 2020, Legal & Disclaimer Notice i

Introduction ii

Alphabet Recognition

    Letter A 1

    Letter B 2

    Letter C 3

    Letter D 4

    Letter E 5

    Letter F 6

    Letter G 7

    Letter H 8

    Letter I 9

    Letter J 10

    Letter K 11

    Letter L 12

    Letter M 13

    Letter N 14

    Letter O 15

    Letter P 16

    Letter Q 17

    Letter R 18

    Letter S 19

    Letter T 20

Table of Contents

Letter U 21

Letter V 22

Letter W 23

Letter X 24

Letter Y 25

Letter Z 26

Consonants & Vowels

Activity 1 27

Activity 2 28

Activity 3 29

Activity 4 30

Activity 5 31

Activity 6 32

Activity 7 33

Activity 8 34

Consonants & Vowels

Activity 1 35

Activity 2 36

Activity 3 37

Activity 4 38

Rhyming Words

Activity 1 39

Activity 2 40

Table of Contents

Activity 3 41

Activity 4 42

Activity 5 43

Activity 6 44

Activity 7 45

Blending & Segmenting

Activity 1 46

Activity 2 47

Activity 3 48

Activity 4 49

Activity 5 50

Activity 6 51

Consonant Sounds and Letters

Activity 1 52

Activity 2 53

Activity 3 54

Activity 4 55

Activity 5 56

Activity 6 57

Activity 7 58

Activity 8 59

Activity 9 60

Activity 10 61

Activity 11 62

Table of Contents

Consonant Blends & Digraphs

- Activity 1 63
- Activity 2 64
- Activity 3 65
- Activity 4 66
- Activity 5 67
- Activity 6 68
- Activity 7 69
- Activity 8 70
- Activity 9 71
- Activity 10 72

Sight Words

- Activity 1 73
- Activity 2 74
- Activity 3 75
- Activity 4 76
- Activity 5 77
- Activity 6 78
- Activity 7 79
- Activity 8 80
- Activity 9 81
- Activity 10 82

Table of Contents

Consonant Blends & Digraphs

- Activity 1 63
- Activity 2 64
- Activity 3 65
- Activity 4 66
- Activity 5 67
- Activity 6 68
- Activity 7 69
- Activity 8 70
- Activity 9 71
- Activity 10 72

Sight Words

- Activity 1 73
- Activity 2 74
- Activity 3 75
- Activity 4 76
- Activity 5 77
- Activity 6 78
- Activity 7 79
- Activity 8 80
- Activity 9 81
- Activity 10 82

Table of Contents

Phonics
Activity 1 83
Activity 2 84
Activity 3 85
Activity 4 86
Activity 5 87
Activity 6 88

Grammar
Activity 1 89
Activity 2 90
Activity 3 91
Activity 4 92
Activity 5 93
Activity 6 94

Vocabulary Word Bank
Activity 1 95
Activity 2 96
Activity 3 97
Activity 4 98
Activity 5 99
Activity 6 100

INTRODUCTION

Dyslexia is a learning disorder. It can be said that a person is dyslexic when they have difficulties reading and understanding what is written. When a child has dyslexia, it is much more difficult to decode the letters and read fluently that is why these children often lose the thread of the class. Dyslexia can be worked to improve the child's reading, writing, and comprehension.

The best way to work on these exercises with your child is to create a routine and work on one or two exercises each day. In this volume, we cover exercises to practice writing with a complementary activity to also practice with the letters learned. Never put excessive pressure on the child. Patience should be our word mantra. Keep in mind that for the child an exercise that you consider easy is very hard for them.

Focus on the child's small advances. Power your effort and less your results. Do everything you can so that they don't feel bad. Keep in mind that the child is making a great effort. When we suspect that our child may be dyslexic, we can do a series of activities that will improve his literacy level. Whether in the end, the diagnosis is confirmed or discarded, it will still be very beneficial to facilitate their learning experience.

The important thing is to carry out this type of training before the age of 8 or 9, preferably during the last year of preschool and the first year of Primary School, without taking into account that from school there is still no warning. In any case, we cannot wait for the diagnosis to be confirmed because we will have missed the best time to intervene and prepare the child to learn to read, and we will have a serious problem if they start 3rd grade and we have not yet intervened the dyslexia, since the increase in school demands will make the problem visible.

In this book and the other volumes of BrainChild, you will find a multitude of resources to work with dyslexia both at school and at home. The exercises have been carried out under the supervision of psychologists and educators.

LETTER RECOGNITION

Color the jars with the letters **A** and **a**

LETTER RECOGNITION

Color the mugs with the letters C and c

LETTER RECOGNITION

Color the clouds with the letters **D** and **d**

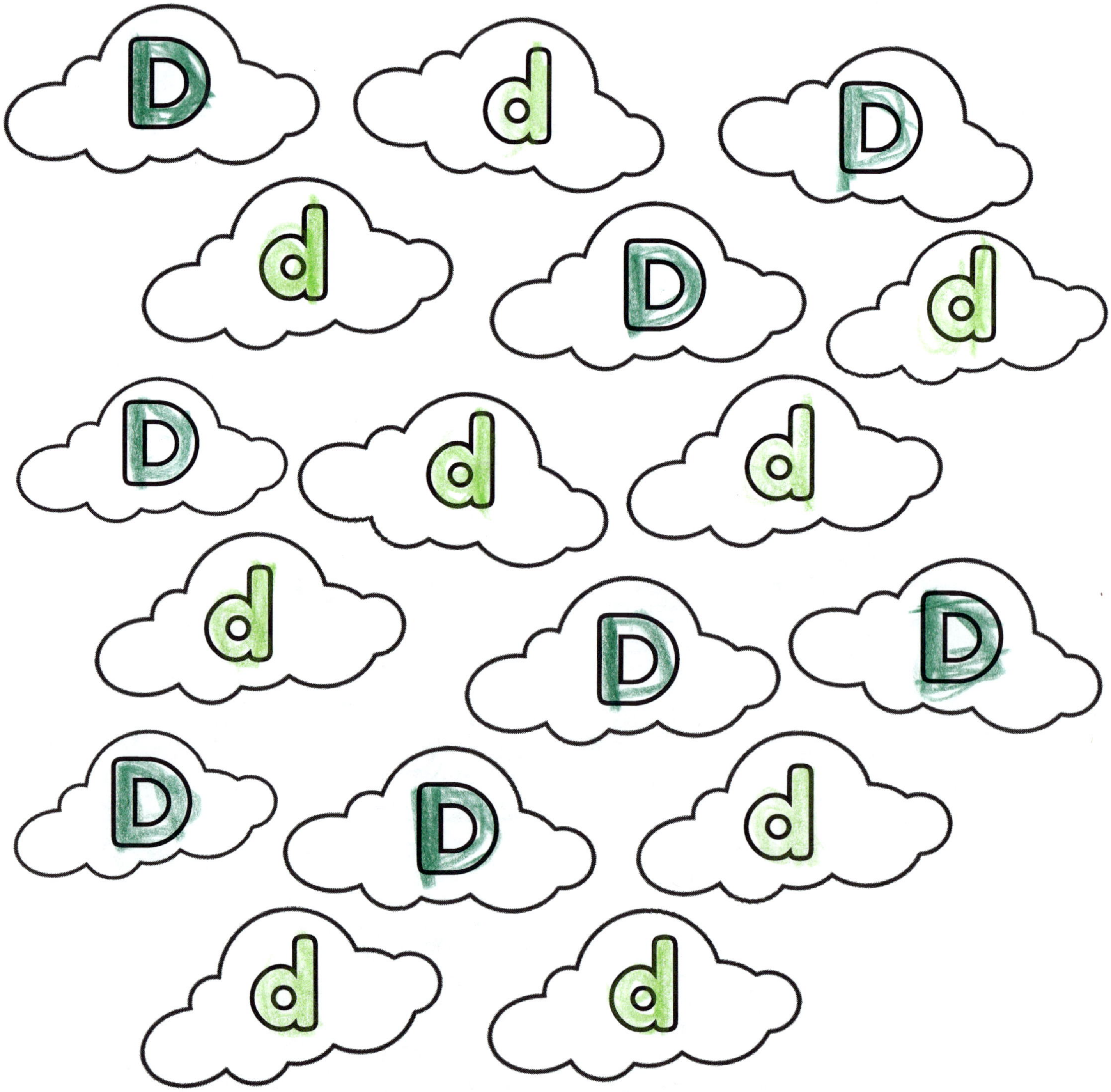

LETTER RECOGNITION

Color the droplets with the letters E and e

LETTER RECOGNITION

Color the ♥ hearts with the letters F and f

LETTER RECOGNITION

Color the ★ stars witht the letters G and g

LETTER RECOGNITION

Color the ♥hearts with the letters H and h

LETTER RECOGNITION

Color the 🌙 moon with the letters I and i

LETTER RECOGNITION

Color the jug with the letters J and j

LETTER RECOGNITION

Color the kettle with the letters **K** and **k**

LETTER RECOGNITION

Color the muffin with the letters **M** and **m**

LETTER RECOGNITION

Color the 🌰 nut with the letters **N** and **n**

LETTER RECOGNITION

Color the ⬡ octagon with the letters O and o

LETTER RECOGNITION

Color the pear with the letters **P** and **p**

LETTER RECOGNITION

Color the ? question mark with the letters Q and q

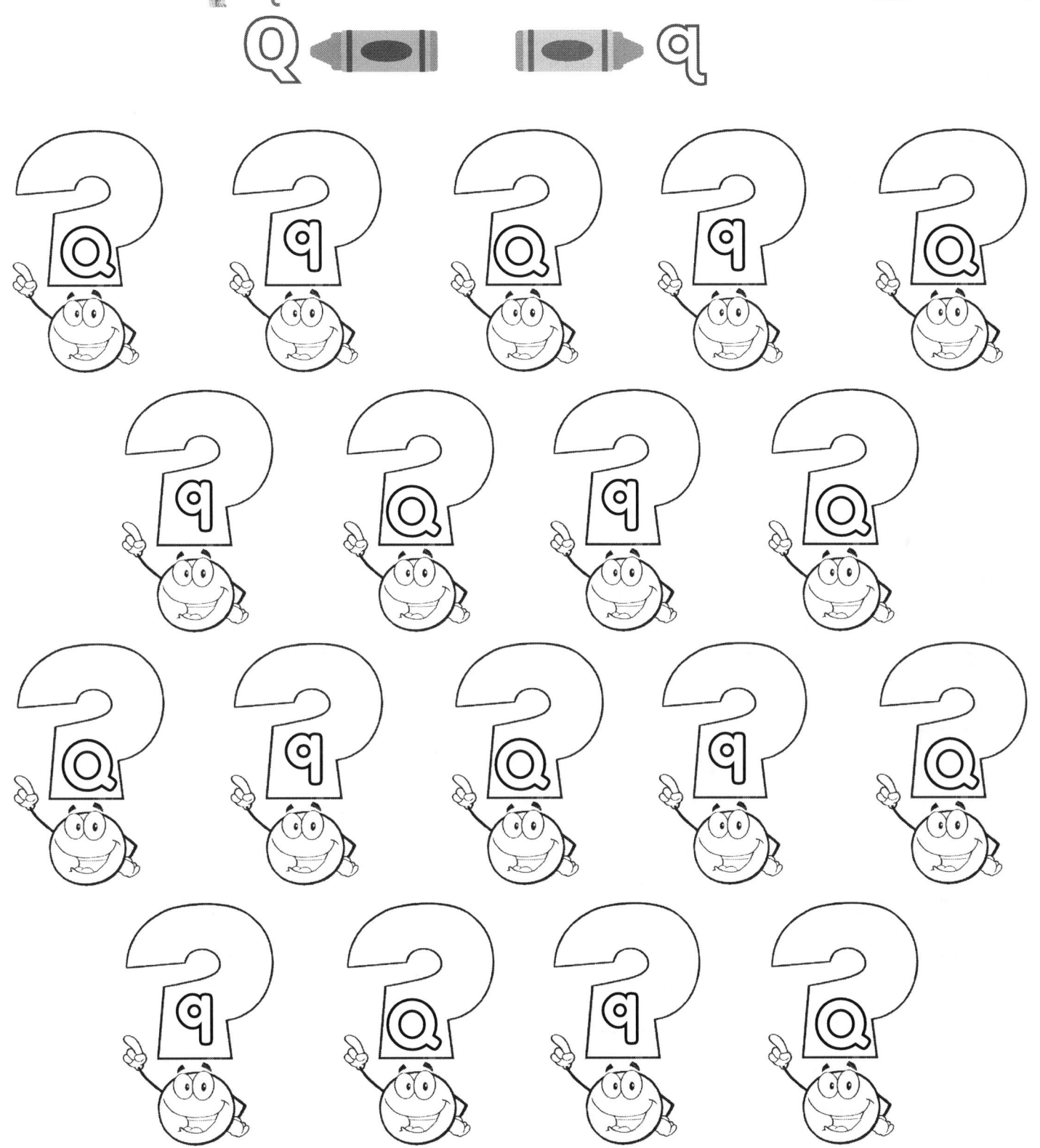

LETTER RECOGNITION

Color the rabbit with the letters **R** and **r**

R r

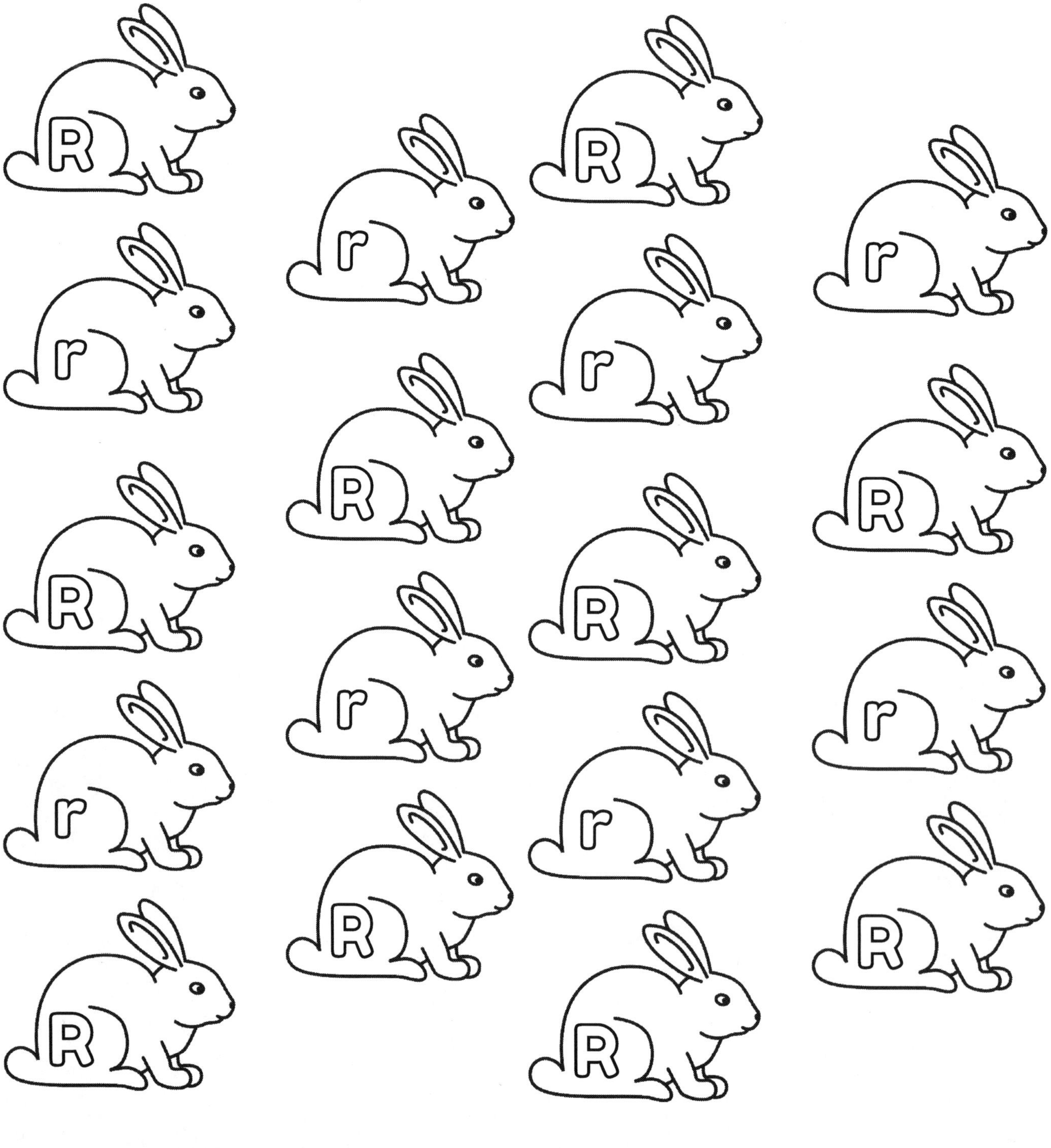

LETTER RECOGNITION

Color the  sun with the letters **S** and **s**

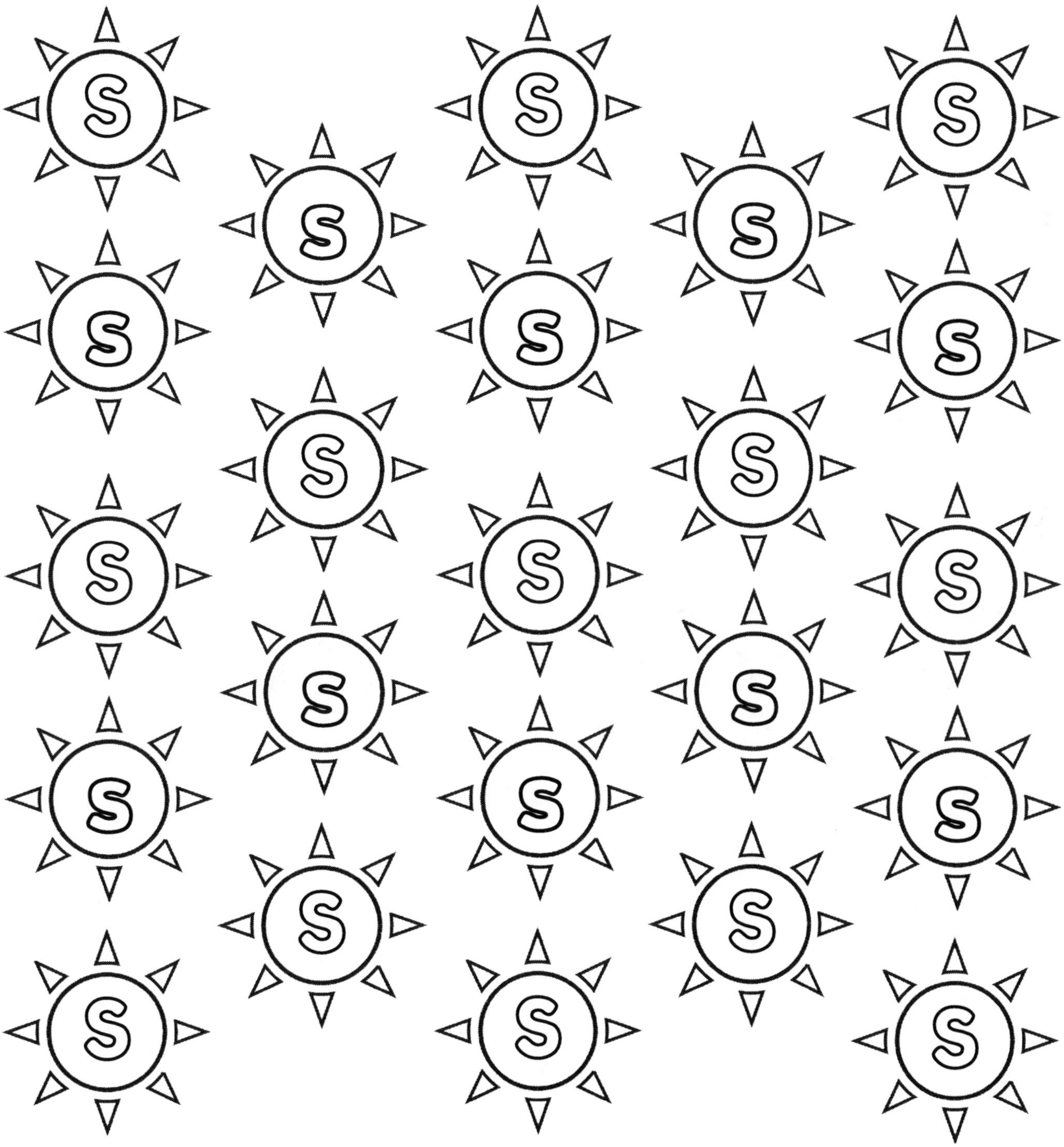

LETTER RECOGNITION

Color the 🦷 tooth with the letters **T** and **t**

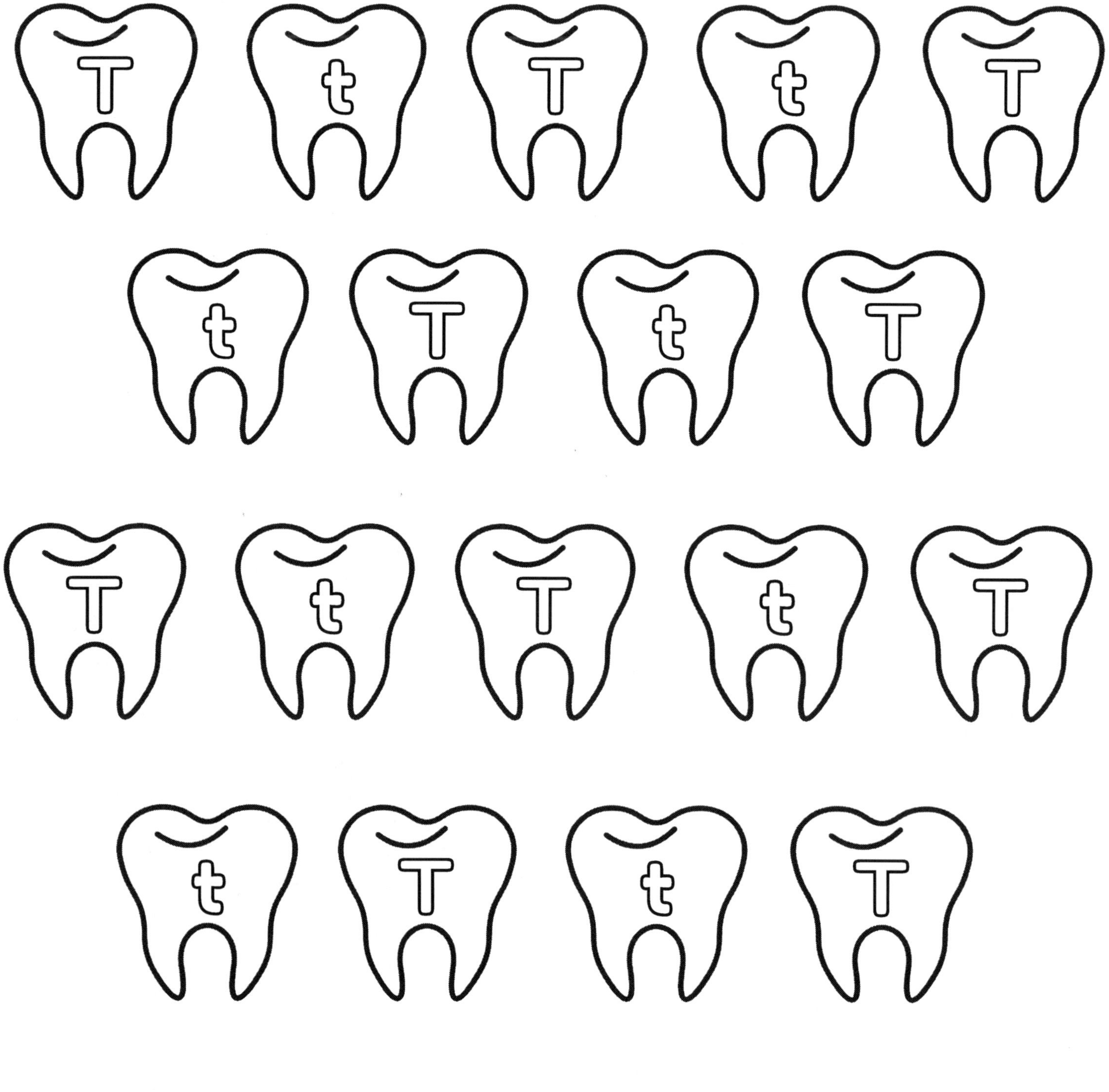

LETTER RECOGNITION

Color the 🔓 lock with the letters **U** and **u**

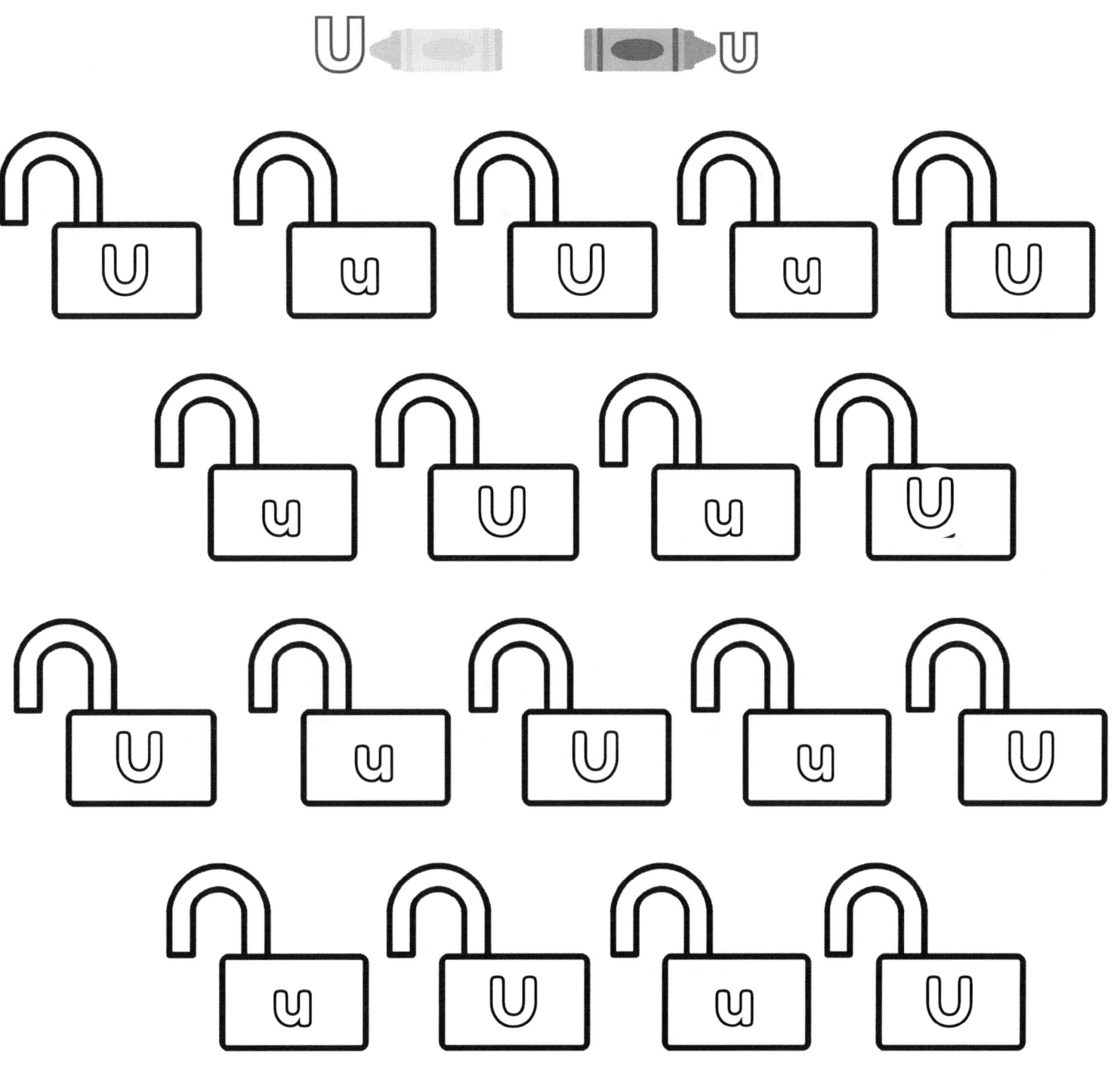

LETTER RECOGNITION

Color the vase with the letters **V** and **v**

LETTER RECOGNITION

Color the  watch with the letters **W** and **w**

LETTER RECOGNITION

Color the xylophone with the letters X and x

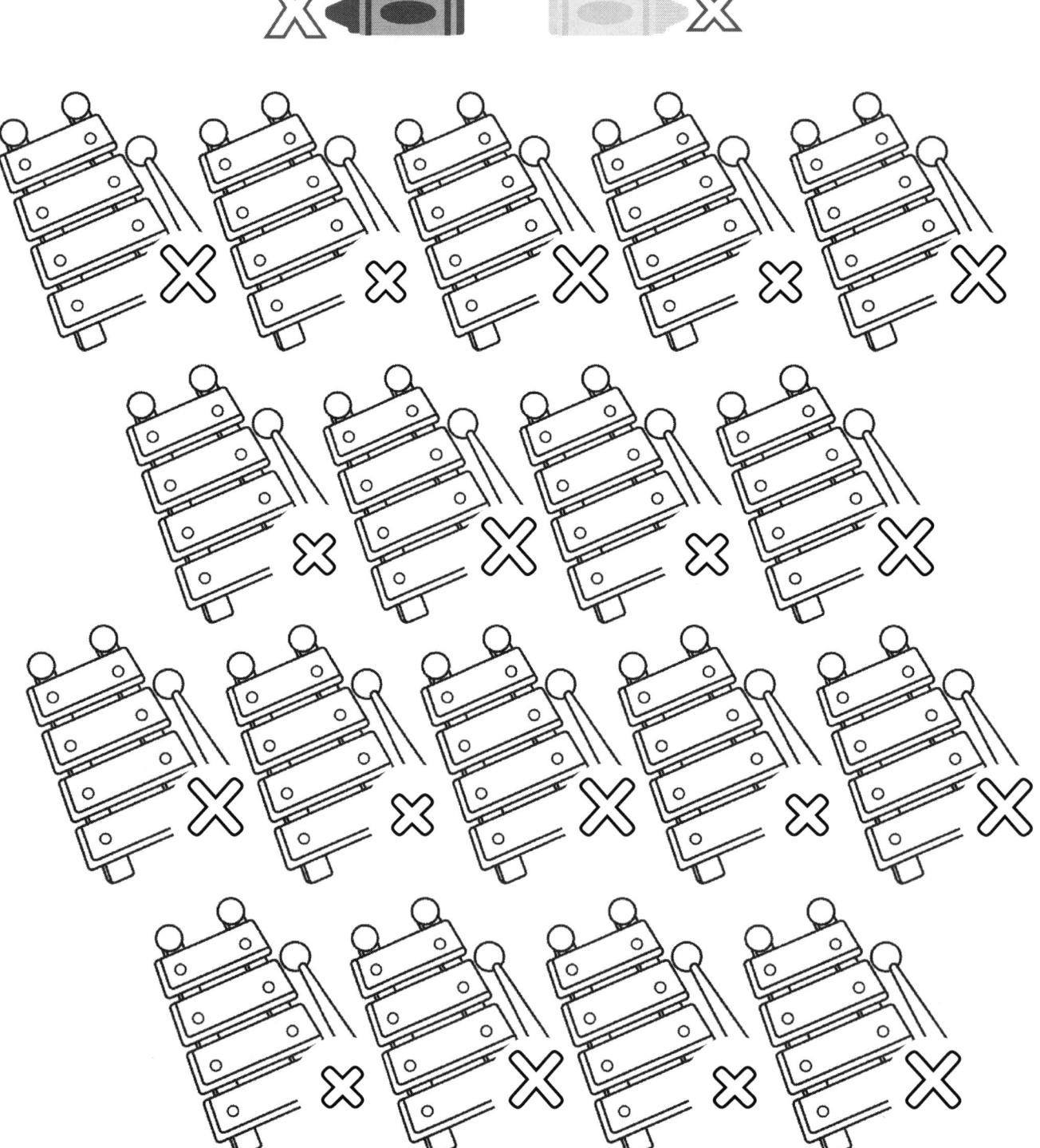

LETTER RECOGNITION

Color the yoyo with the letters Y and y

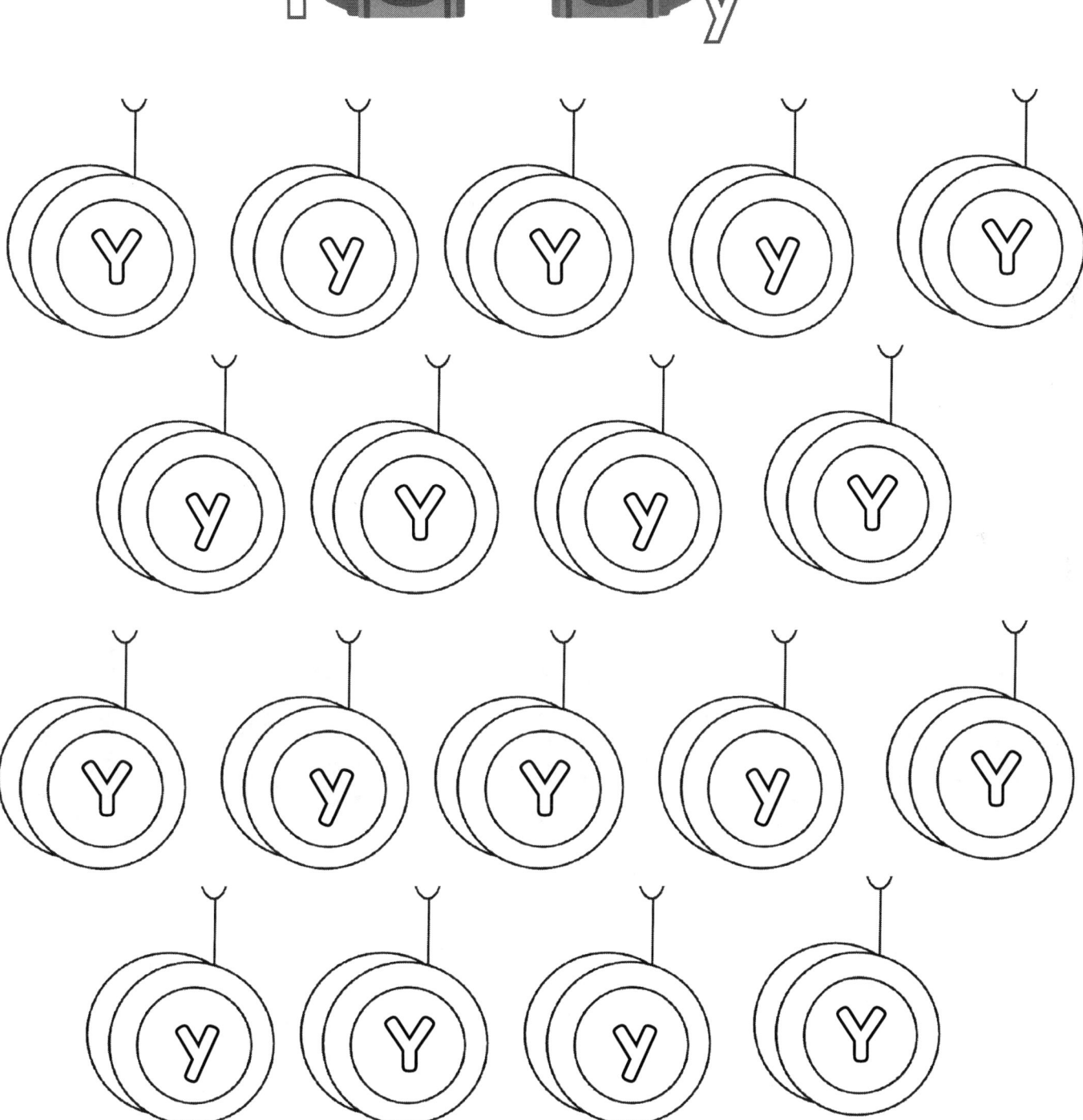

LETTER RECOGNITION

Color the O zero with the letters Z and z

CONSONANTS & VOWELS

Activity 1 — Directions: Sort the letters

1. O T
2. B A
3. Z U
4. F A
5. Q I
6. P E
7. K O
8. L A
9. D I
10. N U

CONSONANTS	VOWELS

CONSONANTS & VOWELS

Activity 2 — Directions: Sort the letters

1. P A V
2. L U X
3. R S O
4. L A U
5. W I S
6. Q U E
7. S T A
8. M I T
9. L E A
10. P C O

CONSONANTS	VOWELS

CONSONANTS & VOWELS

Activity 3 — Directions: Sort the letters

1. P O L I
2. T M A E
3. Y E O L
4. Q A C E
5. P A L W
6. O A T V
7. L M A I
8. C I O A
9. A Z X E
10. F S A E

CONSONANTS	VOWELS

CONSONANTS & VOWELS

Activity 4 — Directions: Sort the letters

1. L W E I V
2. A S D E P
3. M X E F O
4. O I A R T
5. Q S X E I
6. P A E T C
7. O C S P R
8. P X E M V
9. A O U S D
10. P G E I U

CONSONANTS	VOWELS

CONSONANTS & VOWELS

Activity 5 — Directions: Encircle the vowels in the word

1. up
2. on
3. an
4. am
5. if
6. as
7. go
8. of
9. me
10. is
11. at
12. no
13. we
14. to

CONSONANTS & VOWELS

Activity 6 — Directions: Encircle the vowels in the word

1. can
2. bet
3. for
4. yet
5. yes
6. end
7. fix
8. him
9. did
10. bet
11. sum
12. sun
13. got
14. not

CONSONANTS & VOWELS

Activity 7 — Directions: Encircle the vowels in the word

1. what
2. from
3. into
4. they
5. when
6. take
7. with
8. trip
9. jump
10. more
11. them
12. then
13. like
14. this

CONSONANTS & VOWELS

Activity 8 — Directions: Encircle the vowels in the word

1. sheet
2. house
3. stone
4. apple
5. fight
6. clock
7. cabin
8. print
9. paper
10. storm
11. chair
12. child
13. water
14. plant

SYLLABLES

Activity 1 — Directions: Shade how many syllables does the picture have.

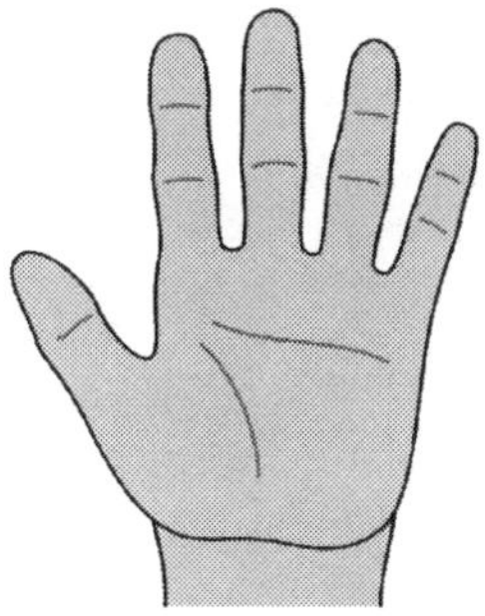

Hand ① ②	Rocket ① ②	Money ① ②	Basket ① ②
Queen ① ②	Bell ① ②	Cookies ① ②	Rabbit ① ②
Peanuts ① ②	Fish ① ②	King ① ②	Jacket ① ②

SYLLABLES

Activity 2 — Directions: Shade how many syllables does the picture have.

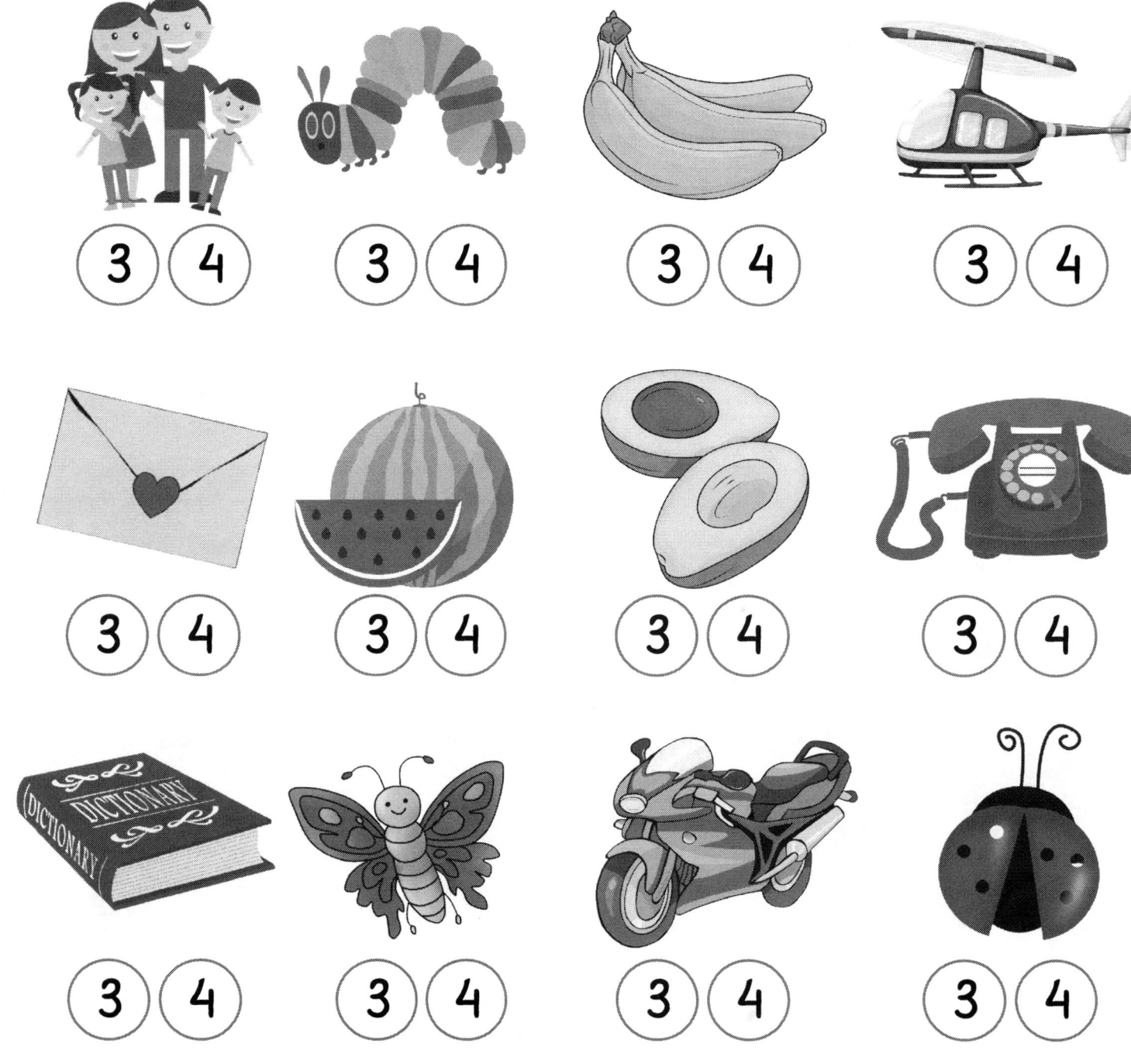

SYLLABLES

Activity 3 — Directions: Box the picture that has more syllables.

  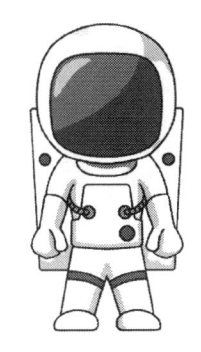 

SYLLABLES

Activity 4

Directions: Box the picture that has more syllables.

RHYMING WORDS

Activity 1

Directions: Circle the word that rhymes.

1. FUN — TOP TEN HOT SUN

2. TOP — FIT MOB POP SET

3. CAT — TIN RAT NUT BUN

4. TIN — SAIL CAT PIN ROAD

5. VET — CAT SET POP BIN

RHYMING WORDS

Activity 2

Directions: Circle the word that rhymes.

1. **FOG** — DOG BED MAN SAT

2. **COW** — FEE DOG RUN HOW

3. **MAD** — LIP TOP HOW SAD

4. **HIT** — BEAT HAT PIT SAT

5. **HAM** — HAS DAM BEAM NET

RHYMING WORDS

Activity 3

Directions: Circle the word that rhymes.

1. TREE — BEAT BEE TRAY TIE

2. WET — FEET WANT NET TEE

3. MUG — BUG BAD BAG MAN

4. DOG — BEG DOLL LOG MUG

5. TEN — HEN NET FED BED

RHYMING WORDS

Activity 4

Directions: Mark (x) the word that **DOES NOT** rhymes.

- TRUCK LUCK TWIN SUCK
- NAP TELL SELL BELL
- BLACK SACK BACK HOT
- SWIM HIM TEN RIM
- RIB BEST NEST VEST

RHYMING WORDS

Activity 5

Directions: Mark (x) the word that **DOES NOT** rhymes.

- LOSS TOSS TRIP BOSS
- THIN DROP TIN BIN
- MOB HID RID BID
- NAG DOT RAG BAG
- ROB SOB HOB CRAB

RHYMING WORDS

Activity 6

Directions: Mark (x) the word that **DOES NOT** rhymes.

- BUMP JUMP SUCH HUMP

- FACE PLACE RACE HAY

- CAVE RAVE SAVE SHARE

- HOT DOT NOT FOR

- SEED FEED WEAK WEED

RHYMING WORDS

Activity 7

Directions: Mark (x) the word that <u>**DOES NOT**</u> rhymes.

- COOK LOOK TOOL HOOK
- BOAT FOLD COAT FLOAT
- RAIN STAY HAY DAY
- HOLE PICK STOLE MOLE
- WILL WALL ALL CALL

BLENDING & SEGMENTING

Activity 1 — Directions: Identify the **first sound** in the word. Shade the correct letter.

D C K   M P N   F L J

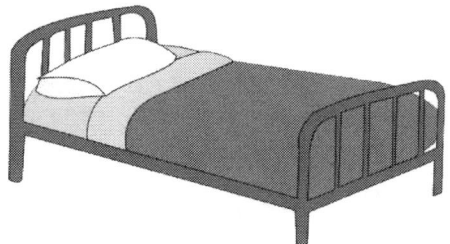

V R B   T B Y   B D T

H S B   C H T   B A H

BLENDING & SEGMENTING

Activity 2 — Directions: Identify the <u>first sound</u> in the word. Shade the correct letter.

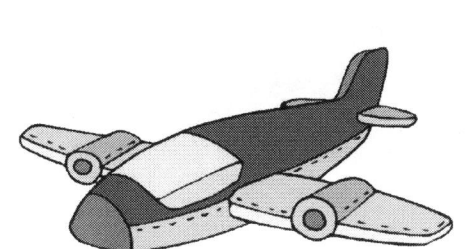

(B) (J) (S)

(B) (L) (D)

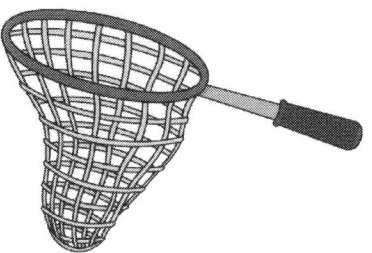

(N) (B) (M)

(P) (F) (C)

(C) (K) (M)

(F) (P) (J)

(F) (P) (B)

(E) (I) (Y)

(I) (O) (E)

47

BLENDING & SEGMENTING

Activity 3 — Directions: Identify the **second sound** in the word. Shade the correct letter.

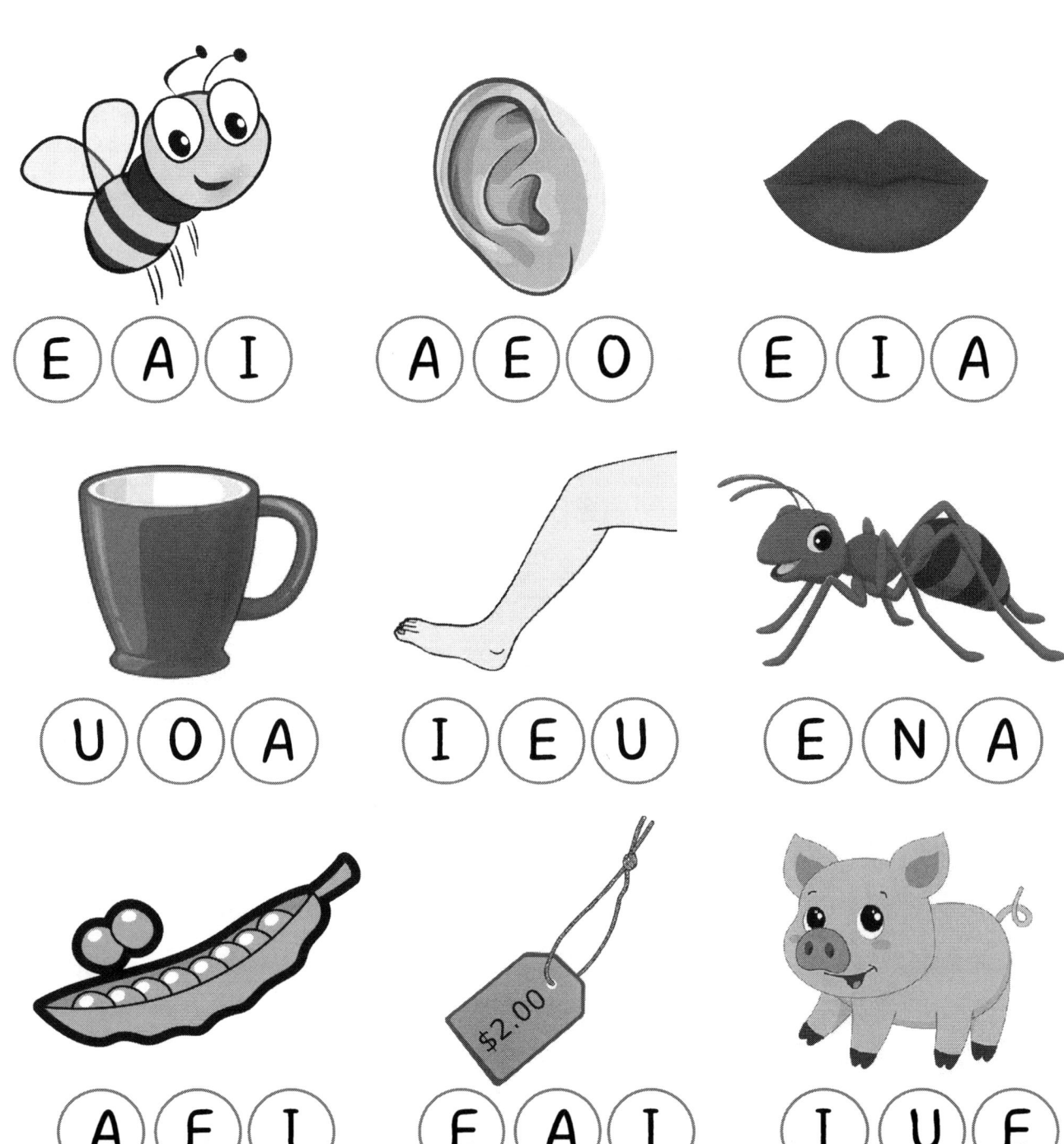

BLENDING & SEGMENTING

Activity 4 — Directions: Identify the **second sound** in the word. Shade the correct letter.

BLENDING & SEGMENTING

Activity 5 — Directions: Identify the **third sound** in the word. Shade the correct letter.

BLENDING & SEGMENTING

Activity 6 Directions: Identify the **third sound** in the word. Shade the correct letter.

N E O

O U T

R A C

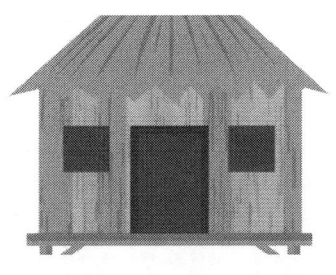
P T H

F T P

N M L

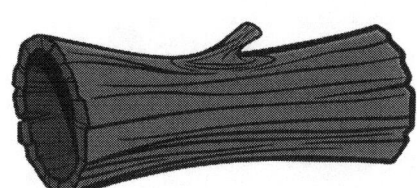
G T L

B E S

B E W

51

CONSONANT SOUNDS & LETTERS

52

Activity 1 Directions: Check (✓) all the pictures that start with the letters **B & C.**

CONSONANT SOUNDS & LETTERS

Activity 2 — Directions: Check (✓) all the pictures that start with the letters **D & F.**

CONSONANT SOUNDS & LETTERS

54

Activity 3 — Directions: Check (✓) all the pictures that start with the letters <u>G & H.</u>

CONSONANT SOUNDS & LETTERS

Activity 4 Directions: Check (✓) all the pictures that start with the letters **J & K**.

CONSONANT SOUNDS & LETTERS

Activity 5 — Directions: Check (✓) all the pictures that start with the letters **L & M.**

CONSONANT SOUNDS & LETTERS

Activity 6 — Directions: Check (✓) all the pictures that start with the letters <u>N & P.</u>

CONSONANT SOUNDS & LETTERS

Activity 7 — Directions: Check (✓) all the pictures that start with the letters **Q & R.**

CONSONANT SOUNDS & LETTERS

Activity 8

Directions: Check (✓) all the pictures that start with the letters **S & T**.

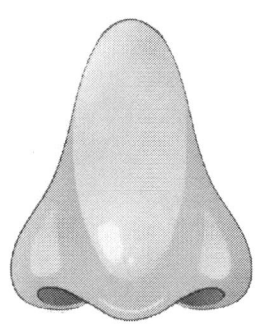

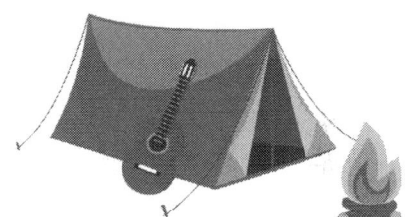

CONSONANT SOUNDS & LETTERS

Activity 9 — Directions: Check (✓) all the pictures that start with the letters <u>U & V.</u>

CONSONANT SOUNDS & LETTERS

Activity 10 Directions: Check (✓) all the pictures that start with the letters <u>W & X</u>

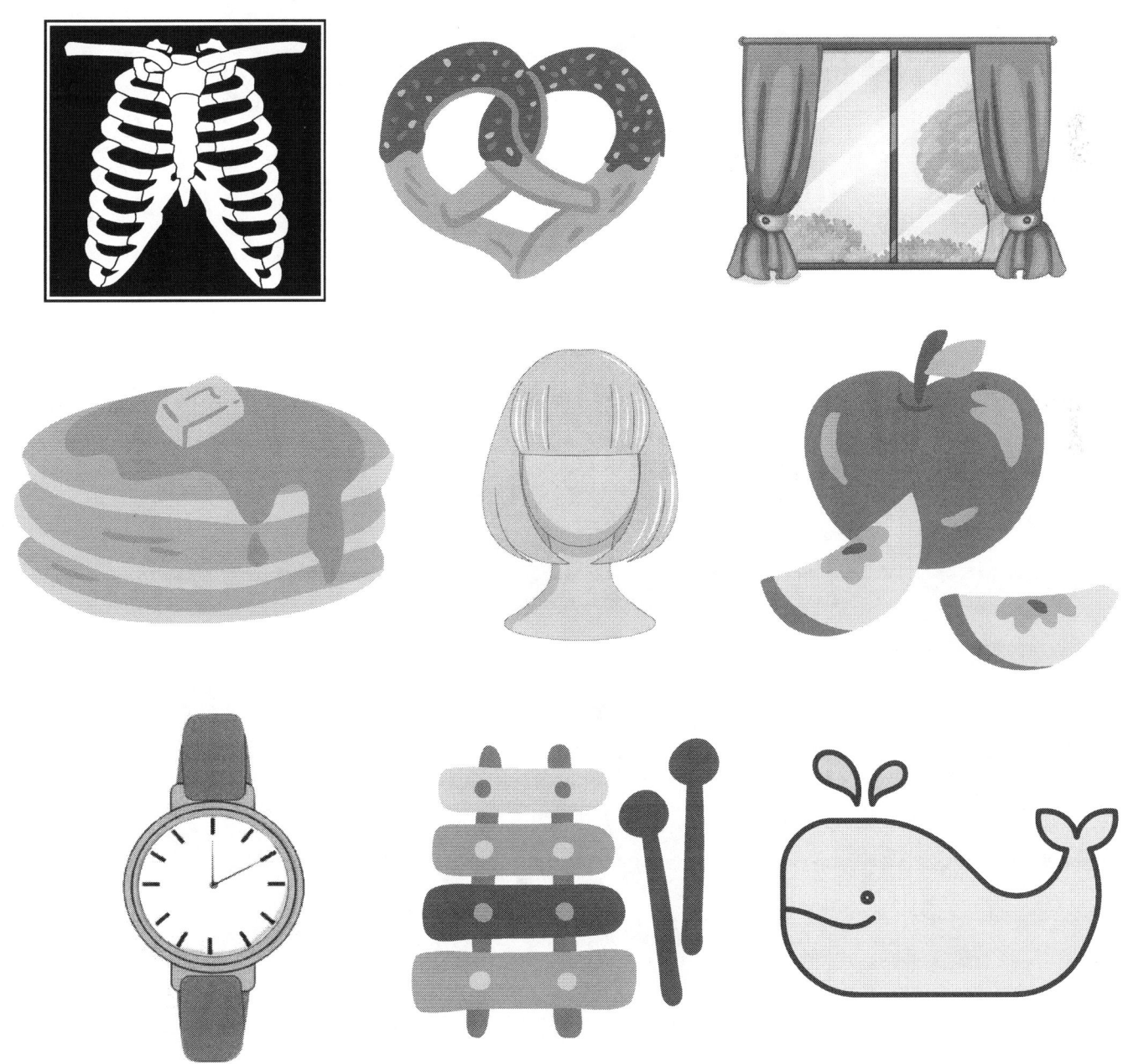

CONSONANT SOUNDS & LETTERS

Activity 11 — Directions: Check (✓) all the pictures that start with the letters **Y & Z**.

CONSONANT BLENDS & DIAGRAPHS

Activity 1

Directions: Match the picture to where its consonant blend starts.

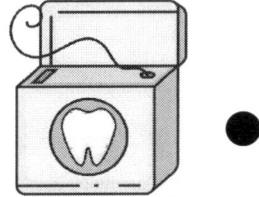

- bl
- br
- cl
- cr
- dr
- fl

CONSONANT BLENDS & DIAGRAPHS

Activity 2

Directions: Match the picture to where its consonant blend starts.

 • • fr

 • • gl

 • • gr

 • • pl

 • • pr

 • • sc

CONSONANT BLENDS & DIAGRAPHS

Activity 3

Directions: Match the picture to where its consonant blend starts.

   •   • sk

   •   • sl

   •   • sm

   •   • sn

   •   • sp

   •   • st

CONSONANT BLENDS & DIAGRAPHS

Activity 4

Directions: Match the picture to where its consonant blend starts.

- sw
- tr
- tw
- wh
- th
- ph

CONSONANT BLENDS & DIAGRAPHS

Activity 5

Directions: Match the picture to where its consonant blend starts.

 •

 •

 •

 •

 •

• screwdriver

• ch

• sh

• str

• scr

• squ

• spr

CONSONANT BLENDS & DIAGRAPHS

Activity 6

Directions: Complete the word to match the picture.

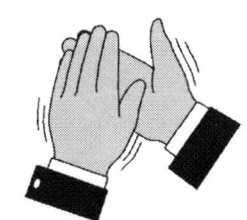 ___ap

 ___y

 ___one

 ___uit

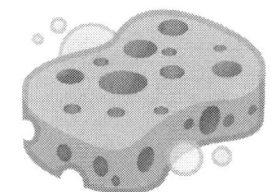 ___onge

 ___obe

 ___an

 ___ower

 ___ime

 ___oes

CONSONANT BLENDS & DIAGRAPHS

Activity 7

Directions: Complete the word to match the picture.

 __umb

 __ell

 __eath

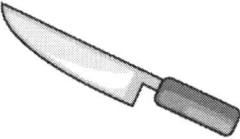 __ife

 __iet

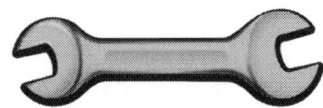 __ench

 __erry

 __eat

 __istle

 __ess

CONSONANT BLENDS & DIAGRAPHS

Activity 8

Directions: Complete the word to match the picture.

 ___ree

 ___ead

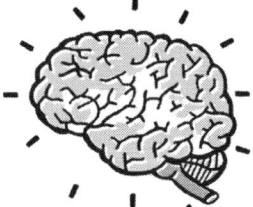 ___ain

 ___irt

 ___icken

 ___ail

 ___ip

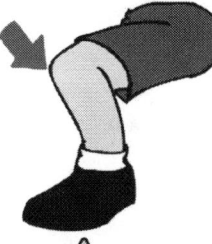 ___ee

 ___eel

 ___rone

CONSONANT BLENDS & DIAGRAPHS

Activity 9

Directions: Complete the word to match the picture.

 du___    ba___

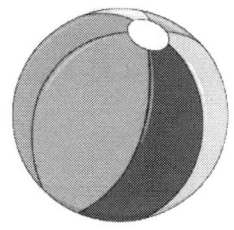 ba___    fi___

 wi___    gi___

 ne___    wa___

 ki___   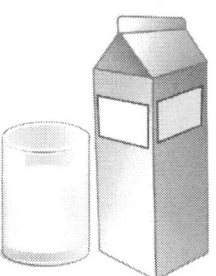 mi___

CONSONANT BLENDS & DIAGRAPHS

Activity 10

Directions: Complete the word to match the picture.

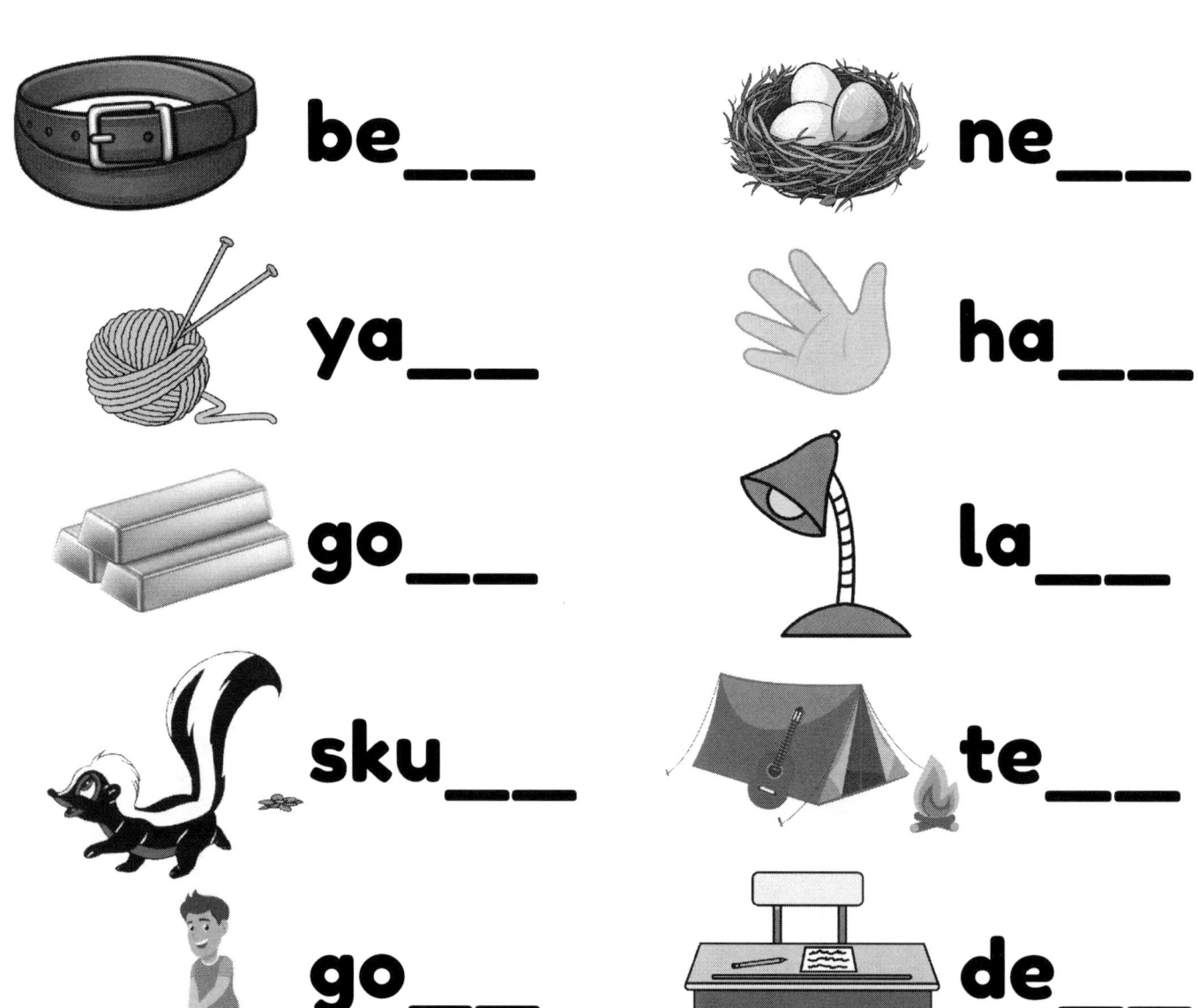

be___   ne___

ya___   ha___

go___   la___

sku___ te___

go___   de___

SIGHT WORDS

Activity 1 — Directions: Read each sentence and box the word that describes the picture.

 The cows produces milk.

 Buttered popcorn smells good

 The chicken lays eggs.

 The rabbit loves the carrot

 The fox is waiting

SIGHT WORDS

Activity 2 — Directions: Read each sentence and box the word that describes the picture.

 The suns shines so bright

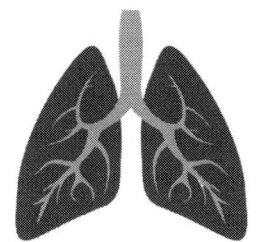 We have two lungs

 I have a stash of cash

 The grill is already set up.

 The dog has spots

SIGHT WORDS

Activity 3 — Directions: Read each sentence and box the word that describes the picture.

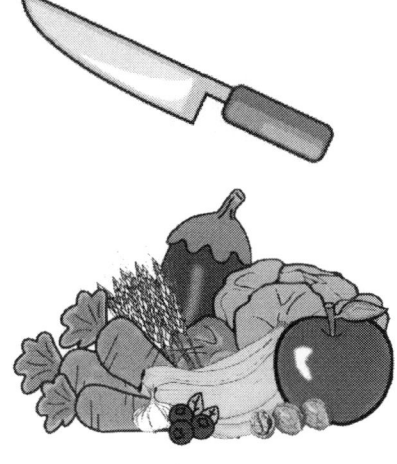

The knife is sharp

The vegetables are fresh

The jar is empty

The volcano erupted

It is healthy to eat fruit

SIGHT WORDS

Activity 4

Directions: Read each sentence and box the word that describes the picture.

Waffles are best for breakfast

Drinking milk is good for bones

The snail moves slow

He is taking a bath

She received a gift

SIGHT WORDS

Activity 5 — Directions: Read each sentence and box the word that describes the picture.

The cat is on the rug

Where is the lamp?

The pen is blue

The mother bought the dress

The shoes are new

SIGHT WORDS

Activity 6

Directions: Trace, Encircle and Finish the sentences with the correct sight words.

Color and trace

We are eating

we we we we we

Find the sight word

We like cookies.

Do we need to ask?

Complete the sentence

_____ have a pet.

SIGHT WORDS

Activity 7 — Directions: Trace, Encircle and Finish the sentences with the correct sight words.

Color and trace

had

She had a great party

had had had had

Find the sight word

I had new shoes

She had nice hair

Complete the sentence

We _____ a tough time

SIGHT WORDS

Activity 8 — Directions: Trace, Encircle and Finish the sentences with the correct sight words.

Color and trace

He answered the call

call call call call call

Find the sight word

Why did you call?

Call me back.

Complete the sentence

_____ the customer service

SIGHT WORDS

Activity 9 — Directions: Trace, Encircle and Finish the sentences with the correct sight words.

Color and trace

must

You must wear a hat

must must must

Find the sight word

You must wear your coat

The man must be tired

Complete the sentence

She _____ be sad.

SIGHT WORDS

Activity 10 — Directions: Trace, Encircle and Finish the sentences with the correct sight words.

Color and trace

I see Anna eating apples

see see see see see

Find the sight word

Can you see the house?
I can see the horse.

Complete the sentence

Did you _____ the shooting star?

PHONICS

Activity 1

Directions: Circle the correct beginning sound of the picture

a y o

m e p

a m e

f e p

a e s

t e c

a e o

t e w

r e p

PHONICS

Activity 2

Directions: Circle the correct beginning sound of the picture

s c e

a p o

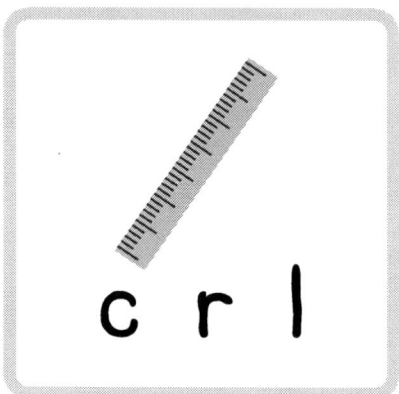
c r l

b e o

p e w

a b l

p g j

a e c

a s w

PHONICS

85

Activity 3

Directions: Circle the correct beginning sound of the picture

l d o

f e s

l f c

p o u

a s m

f m o

m i o

p e d

p l k

PHONICS

Activity 4

Directions: Write the correct short vowel sound to complete the word

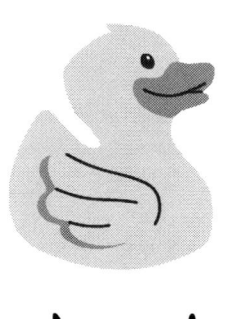
d_ck

d_g

_wl

v_n

s_n

f_sh

l_g

t_n

p_g

PHONICS

Activity 5 — Directions: Write the correct short vowel sound to complete the word

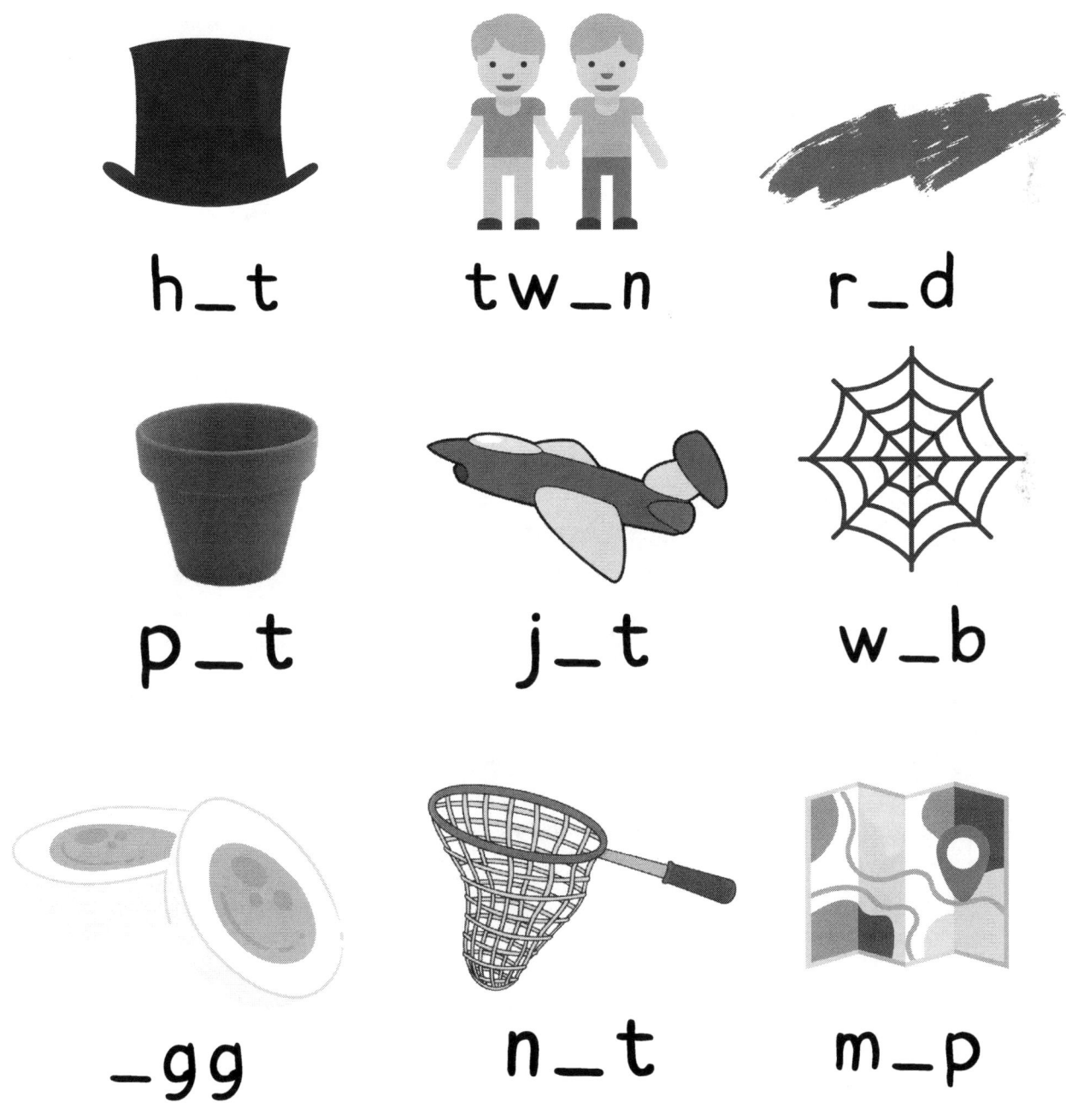

h_t   tw_n   r_d

p_t   j_t   w_b

_gg   n_t   m_p

87

PHONICS

Activity 6

Directions: Write the correct short vowel sound to complete the word

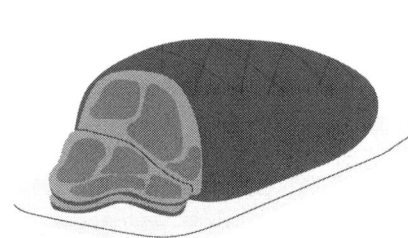
h_m

n_t

c_p

b_x

c_p

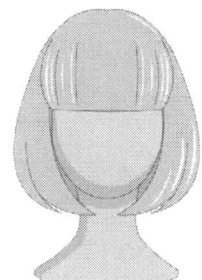
w_g

m_d

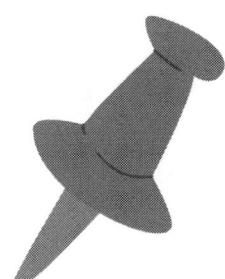
p_n

k_d

GRAMMAR

Activity 1 — Directions: Color the box **red** if the given word is a noun and **orange** if it is a verb

ask	verb	noun
boy	verb	noun
arrive	verb	noun
close	verb	noun
mall	verb	noun

GRAMMAR

Activity 2 — Directions: Color the box **red** if the given word is a noun and **orange** if it is a verb

pen	verb	noun
flag	verb	noun
confess	verb	noun
flower	verb	noun
cheer	verb	noun

GRAMMAR

Activity 3 — Directions: Color the box **red** if the given word is a noun and **orange** if it is a verb

challenge	verb	noun
car	verb	noun
run	verb	noun
avoid	verb	noun
princess	verb	noun

GRAMMAR

Activity 4 — Directions: Color the box **red** if the given word is a noun and **orange** if it is a verb

king	verb	noun
girl	verb	noun
walk	verb	noun
cut	verb	noun
mat	verb	noun

GRAMMAR

Activity 5

Directions: Color the box **red** if the given word is a noun and **orange** if it is a verb

call	verb	noun
chew	verb	noun
ocean	verb	noun
blink	verb	noun
nest	verb	noun

GRAMMAR

Activity 6 — Directions: Color the box **red** if the given word is a noun and **orange** if it is a verb

potato	verb	noun
kite	verb	noun
argue	verb	noun
ice	verb	noun
allow	verb	noun

VOCABULARY

Activity 1 — Directions: Read the word in the word bank. Match the picture in the box with the word by writing the number in the circle.

1 = RABBIT 2 = HEART 3 = BAG 4 = SUN
5 = TURTLE 6 = TOOTH 7 = PENCIL 8 = SNAKE

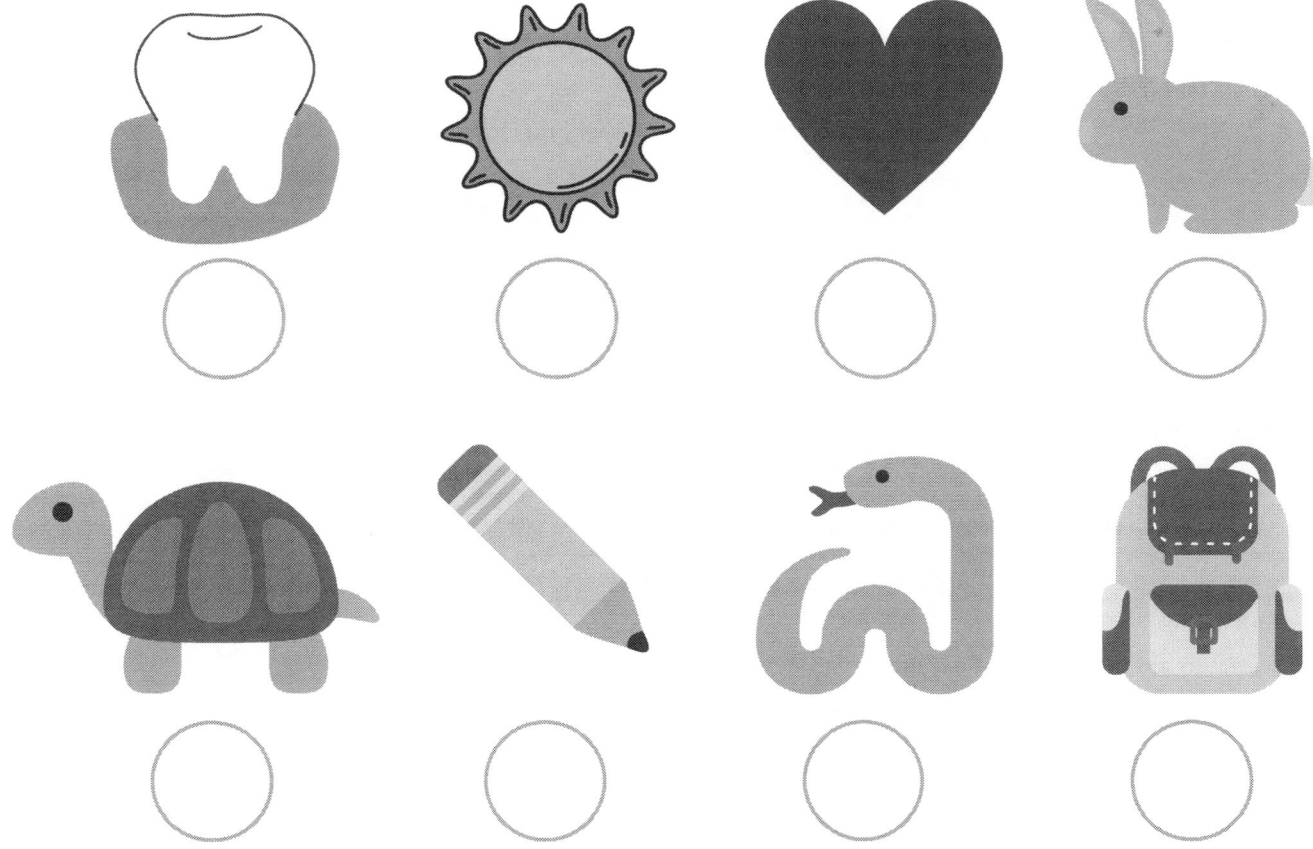

VOCABULARY

Activity 2

Directions: Read the word in the word bank. Match the picture in the box with the word by writing the number in the circle.

1= BUTTER 2= BROCOLLI 3= CHEESE 4= MEAT
5= GLOBE 6= EGG 7= OWL 8= SLIPPERS

VOCABULARY

Activity 3

Directions: Read the word in the word bank. Match the picture in the box with the word by writing the number in the circle.

1 = BEE   2 = SCISSORS   3 = FROG   4 = COW
5 = CRAYONS   6 = CLOUD   7 = TREE   8 = RAINBOW

VOCABULARY

Activity 4

Directions: Read the word in the word bank. Match the picture in the box with the word by writing the number in the circle.

> 1= CAR   2= ANT   3= BLOCKS   4= BIKE
> 5= BUTTERFLY   6= BUG   7= CASH   8= BALL

VOCABULARY

Activity 5

Directions: Read the word in the word bank. Match the picture in the box with the word by writing the number in the circle.

1= TRAIN   2= UMBRELLA   3= PUZZLE   4= TEDDY
5= DOLL   6= ROBOT   7= KITE   8= SHADES

VOCABULARY

Activity 6

Directions: Read the word in the word bank. Match the picture in the box with the word by writing the number in the circle.

> 1= BANANA 2= PRETZEL 3= APPLE 4= JUICE
> 5= MUFFIN 6= PIZZA 7= DONUT 8= WAFFLE

OTHER BRAINCHILD BOOKS AVAILABLE ON AMAZON

Manufactured by Amazon.ca
Bolton, ON

38071438R00063